Online Interactive Student Book

www.macmillanmh.com

StudentWorks *Plus*™

Interactive Student Book

VIEW IT 👁

- Preview weekly concepts and selections

READ IT 📖

- Word-by-Word Reading

LEARN IT 🖱

- Comprehension Questions
- Research and Media Activities
- Grammar, Spelling, and Writing Activities

FIND OUT 🖱

- Summaries and Glossary in other Languages

Online Activities
www.macmillanmh.com

- **Interactive activities** and **animated lessons** for guided instruction and practice

 IWB Interactive White Board Ready!

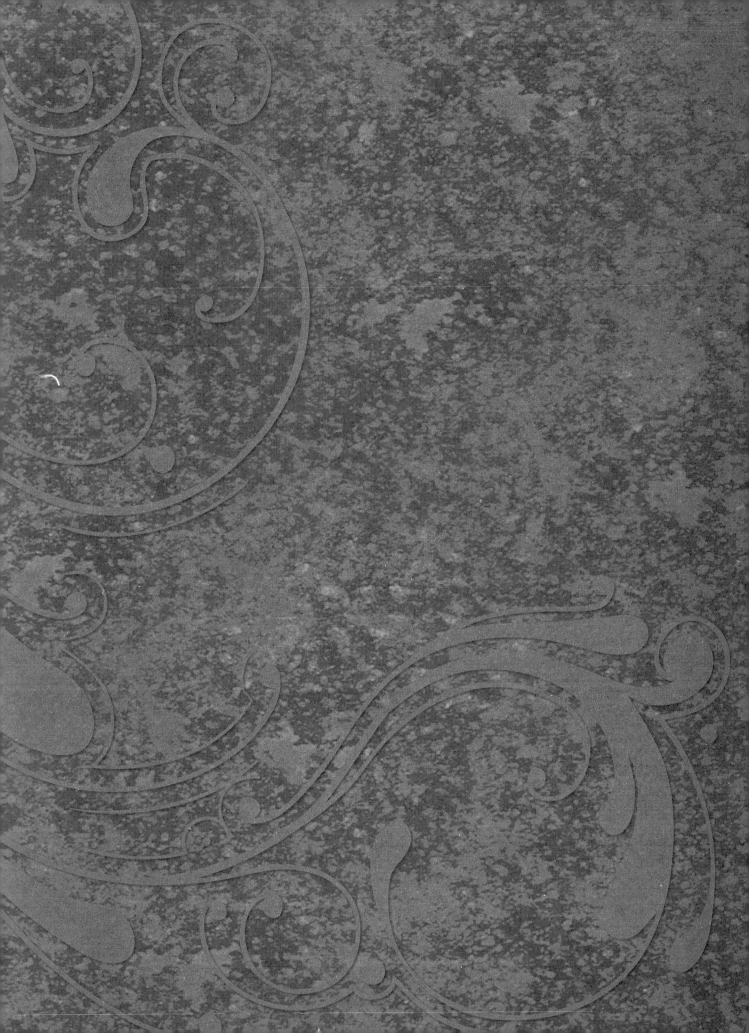

A Reading/Language Arts Program

Macmillan/McGraw-Hill

Contributors

Time Magazine, Accelerated Reader

learning through listening

Students with print disabilities may be eligible to obtain an accessible, audio version of the pupil edition of this textbook. Please call Recording for the Blind & Dyslexic at 1-800-221-4792 for complete information.

B

 The McGraw·Hill Companies

Macmillan/McGraw-Hill

Published by Macmillan/McGraw-Hill, of McGraw-Hill Education, a division of The McGraw-Hill Companies, Inc., Two Penn Plaza, New York, New York 10121.

Printed in the United States of America

ISBN: 978-0-02-201727-9
MHID: 0-02-201727-5

2 3 4 5 6 7 8 9 DOW 13 12 11 10

Treasures

A Reading/Language Arts Program

Program Authors

Diane August
Donald R. Bear
Janice A. Dole
Jana Echevarria
Douglas Fisher
David Francis
Vicki Gibson
Jan E. Hasbrouck
Scott G. Paris
Timothy Shanahan
Josefina V. Tinajero

Macmillan/McGraw-Hill

Creative Expression
Have Fun!

The Big Question

THEME: Let's Laugh

THEME: Family Fun

The
Big
Question

How can we
have fun?

LOG ON ▶ VIEW IT

Theme Video
Have Fun
www.macmillanmh.com

How can we have fun?

If you could do anything you wanted, what would you do? Would you make something out of paper or blocks? Would you read a book or kick a ball? Or would you just sit under a tree and daydream? There are lots of ways to have fun. What makes you and your friends laugh? What makes kids from around the world laugh? How do you have fun?

Research Activities

Make a joke and riddle book. Ask family or friends to share their favorite jokes. Write one down. Draw a picture to go with it. Put all your jokes and riddles together into a class book.

Keep Track of Ideas

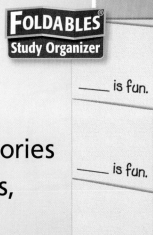
FOLDABLES®
Study Organizer

As you read, keep track of different kinds of fun on the **Three-Tab Foldable**. Use categories such as Games, Making Things, or Being Silly. Draw and write about each kind of fun.

_____ is fun.

_____ is fun.

_____ is fun.

Digital Learning

  www.macmillanmh.com

StudentWorks Plus
Interactive Student Book

- **Research Roadmap**
  Follow a step-by-step guide to complete your research project.

Online Resources
- Topic Finder and Other Research Tools
- Videos and Virtual Field Trips
- Photos and Drawings for Presentations
- Related Articles and Web Resources
- Web Site Links

People and Places

The National Museum of the American Indian

This museum in Washington, D.C., features art and informational exhibits relating to Native Americans past and present.

What makes you laugh? How do you make other people laugh?

LOG ON VIEW IT

Oral Language Activities
Let's Laugh
www.macmillanmh.com

Let's Laugh

Jane Is Late!

☑ **Words to Know**

why
school
today
away
way

_____

Jane

late

Read To Find Out
Why is Jane late?

Why is Jane late to **school today**?
She wants to see some frogs at play.

8

The frogs hop up and hop **away**.
They make Jane very late today!

Why is Jane late on the **way** back?
She wants to see the ducks that quack.

The ducks are glad to see Jane, too.
They are quacking, "We like you!"

Comprehension

Genre
In a **Rhyming Story**, some words end with the same sounds.

Story Structure
✔ **Retell**
Use your Retelling Chart.

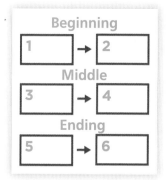

Beginning
1 → 2
Middle
3 → 4
Ending
5 → 6

Read to Find Out
What happens to the boy on his way to school?

On My Way to School

by Wong Herbert Yee

Award Winning Author and Illustrator

On my **way** to **school today**,
a pig asks me to come and play.

It's not just a pig.
It's a pig in a wig!
We run for the bus,
just the two of us.

Pig and I run fast, fast, fast!
We get on the bus at last.
Huff, puff! The bus zips **away**.
Pig makes me late for school today!

On my way to school, we pass
a trash truck that ran out of gas.
On top of that truck,
sit two apes and a duck!

Apes and a duck hop in the bus.
They sit down with the rest of us.

Slip, flip! The bus zips away.
Apes make me late for school today!

On my way to school, I see
frogs up in a gumdrop tree.

Plip, plop! The gumdrops drop.
Two frogs cut. Two frogs mop.

Frogs hop in the bus.

They sit down with the rest of us.

Hip! Hop! The bus zips away.

Frogs make me late for school today!

Here we go, just one last stop.
Frogs hop in the lake. Plip, plop!

Duck is off to get some gas.
Apes fish and nap in the grass.

Tick, tock! The bus zips away.
It looks like I am late today!

Now the bus drops me off at school.
I see a crocodile slink out of a pool!

I think it slid under the gate.
And that, Miss Blake, is **why** I am late!

On the Way with Wong Herbert Yee

Wong Herbert Yee says, "No bus picked me up at the corner. I walked a mile to get to school! When I write, I use things that really happened. My imagination fills in the rest. Remember what you see, read, and hear. You may write a funny story, too!"

Other books by Wong Herbert Yee

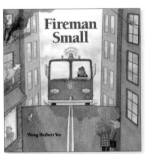

LOG ON ▶ FIND OUT
Author Wong Herbert Yee
www.macmillanmh.com

✔ Author's Purpose

Wong Herbert Yee wanted to write a funny story about getting to school. Draw how you get to school. Write about it.

✔ Comprehension Check

Retell the Story

Use the Retelling Cards to retell the story in order.

Retelling Cards

Think and Compare

Beginning
1 → 2
Middle
3 → 4
Ending
5 → 6

1. What does the pig ask the boy to do?

2. What makes the boy late in the beginning? What makes him late in the middle?

3. What can you tell about the boy from the story?

4. How are *On My Way to School* and "Jane Is Late!" alike?

Social Studies

Genre
Nonfiction gives information about a topic.

✔ **Text Feature**
A Sign uses words or pictures to give information.

Content Vocabulary
signs
symbols
maps

Social Studies Signs and Symbols
www.macmillanmh.com

Signs We See

STOP

What helps you get to school?
Signs, **symbols**, and **maps** help kids get to school.

STOP

SCHOOL XING

CROSSING AHEAD

30

Zack walks to school. He sees
signs on the way. Some signs have
symbols on them. The signs help
Zack get to school safely.

Jake rides the bus to school. The bus driver sees signs on the way. Some signs have words on them. The signs help the bus driver get to school safely.

Pam's mother drives her to a new school today. She looks at a map. The map shows where the school is.

Signs, symbols, and maps help us get to where we want to go safely and easily.

 Connect and Compare

- What signs and symbols do you see in this piece? What do they tell you?
- What signs and symbols might the bus pass in *On My Way to School*?

Write a Silly Poem

Writing

✔ Verbs

A **verb** is a word that names an action.

Callie wrote a silly poem about a cat.

Lots of cats jump and run.

My cat reads just for fun.

Your Turn

Think of something silly.

Write a rhyme about it.

Use an action word.

Grammar and Writing

- Read Callie's poem.
  Point to the verbs.
  Say aloud the words that rhyme.

- Check your poem.
  Do some words rhyme?
  Does each sentence have a verb?

- Read your poem to a partner.

Family Fun

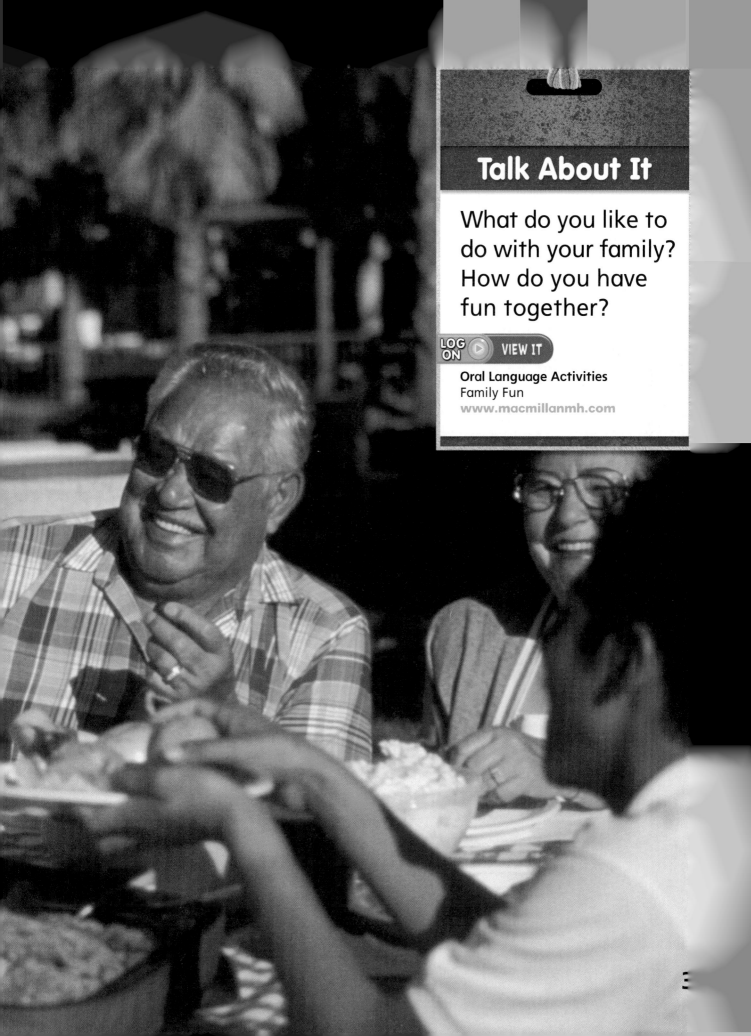

Talk About It

What do you like to do with your family? How do you have fun together?

LOG ON ▶ **VIEW IT**

Oral Language Activities
Family Fun
www.macmillanmh.com

A Dog For Ike

✓ Words to Know

how
there
so
more
funny
call

time
fine

Read To Find Out
What dog will Ike pick out?

Ike: **How** will I pick the best dog? **There** are **so** many dogs in the shop!

Dad: Take some time. You will see one that you like **more** than the rest.

 **Ike:** I like this **funny** dog!
I think it likes me, too!

 **Mom:** Then this must be the
one you want.

 **Mom:** He looks like a fine dog.
Let's get him.

 **Ike:** Let's **call** him Wags!

Comprehension

Genre
A **Play** is a story that can be acted out.

Story Structure
✔ **Make Predictions**
Use your **Predictions Chart.**

What I Predict	What Happens

Read to Find Out
Who will make Mike smile?

Smile, Mike!
A Play

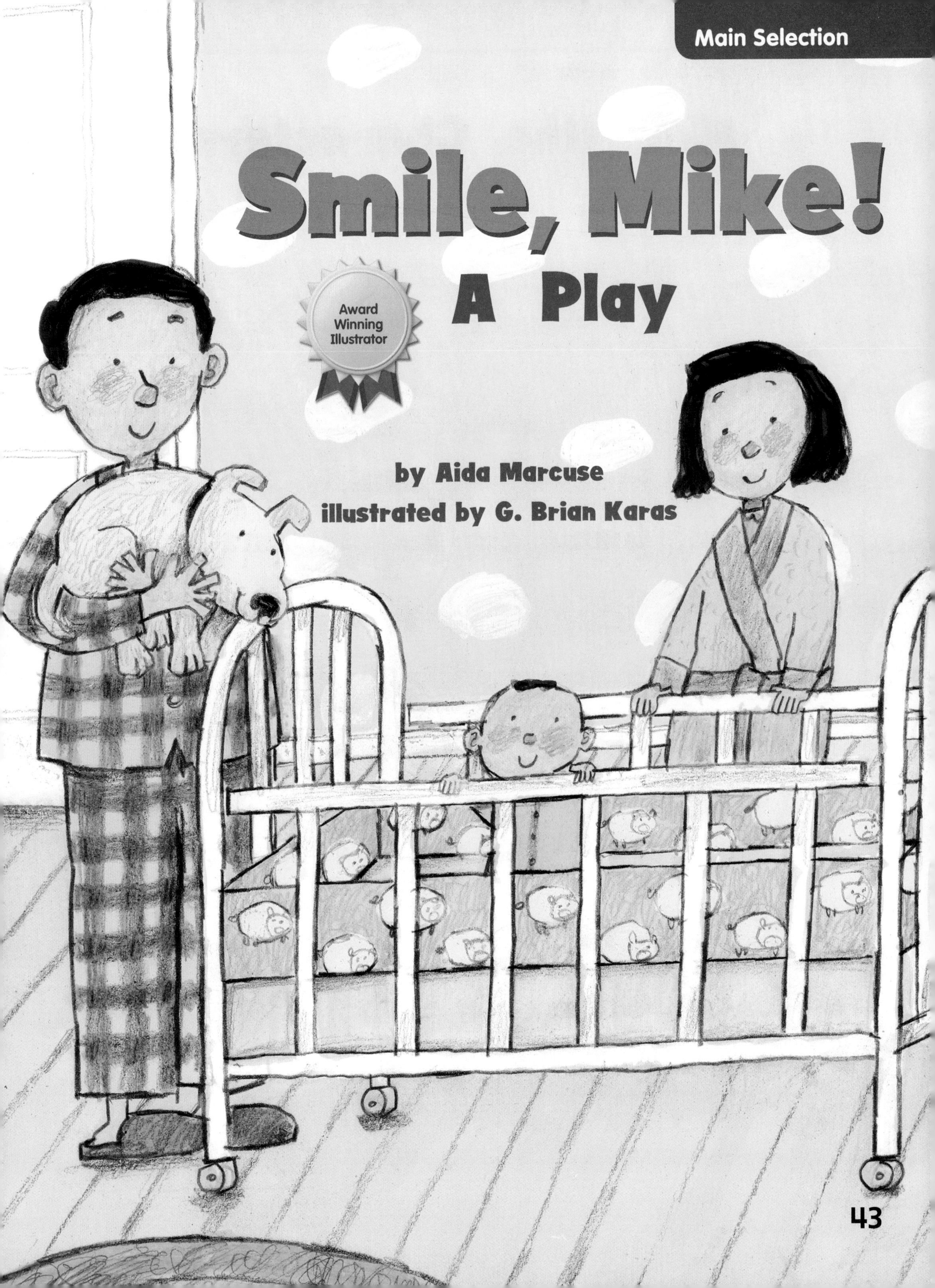

Award Winning Illustrator

by Aida Marcuse

illustrated by G. Brian Karas

Meet the Characters

 Mike

 Spike

 Juan

 Ana

 Mom

 Dad

 Gram

 Pops

 Mike: Waaaah!

 Mom: Here we are, little Mike.

 Dad: Did you **call** us?
Do you want to eat?

 Mom: No, he just had a fine snack.

 Mike: Waaaah!

 Ana: Why is Mike **so** sad?

 Juan: Let's make him happy.
Do you want this cat, Mike?

 Mike: No! No! No cat!

 Ana: Let's sing. A - B - C - D - E - F - G - H - I -

 Dad: J - K - L - M - N - O - P -

 Juan: Q - R - S - T - U - V - W - X - Y - Z.

 Mike: No! No! No sing!

 Gram: Why is our little Mike so sad?

 Mike: Waaaah!

 Pops: **How** can we make him smile?

 Gram: Let's clap hands!

48

 Pops: Clap with us, Mike.

 Mike: Waaah!

 Gram: Clap hands with us.

 Mike: No! No! No clap!

 Ana: This **funny** duck will make Mike smile.

 Mike: Waaah!

 Mom: Do not be sad, Mike. Quack with us. Quack! Quack!

 Mike: No! No! No quack!

 Dad: Look, Mike! I can make bubbles!

 Mike: Waaah!

 Gram: And I can get a bubble.

 Mike: No! No! No bubbles!

 Ana: Mike, look at my funny duck.

 Mike: Waaah!

 Juan: And look at my little cat.

52

 Gram: Look at me, Mike.

 Mike: Waaah!

 Dad: Look! **There** are **more** bubbles!

 Pops: Look, Mike! There is Spike.

 Mike: Waaah!

 Juan: Did you come to see Mike, Spike?

 Ana: Spike wants to make Mike smile.

54

 Gram: Look at Spike spin.

 Ana: Spike is funny!

 Gram: Look! Mike has a big smile.

 Pops: Spike made Mike smile.

55

 Juan: Good dog! This is for you, Spike.

 Dad: Show us how you can jump.

 Mike: Jump, Spike! Jump!

 Spike: Ruff! Ruff!

56

 Dad: At last, Mike is happy.

 Mom: Now it is time for bed.

 Ana: Mike will get some rest now.

 Gram: And so will we!

Smile with Aida Marcuse!

Aida Marcuse says, "I wrote *Smile, Mike!* because mothers always try to make their children happy. I remember the day when my little boy wouldn't stop crying. At last we discovered what he wanted! I hope you enjoy reading this play. I enjoyed writing it!"

LOG ON ▶ FIND OUT

Author Aida Marcuse
www.macmillanmh.com

✔ Author's Purpose

Aida Marcuse wanted to write about making a sad boy smile. What makes you smile? Write about it.

Comprehension Check

Retell the Story

Use the Retelling Cards
to retell the story in order.

Retelling Cards

Think and Compare

What I Predict	What Happens

1. What is Mike doing in the beginning of the story?

2. How does the family try to get Mike to stop crying?

3. What did you predict would happen when Spike came into the room? Why did you predict that? Were you correct?

4. How is Wags, in "A Dog for Ike," like Spike?

59

Healthy Eating

What are some foods your family likes to eat?

My family likes to eat **healthful foods**. Healthful foods give us **energy** to walk, work, and have fun.

Grains **Vegetables** **Fruits** **Milk** **Meat and Beans**

Mom and Dad buy foods that are good for our family to eat. They pick healthful foods like milk, bread, meat, fish, fruits, and vegetables. Grains give us energy. Meat and fish help our muscles grow.

My family likes to help
cook our food. I like to wash the
vegetables. Grandmother chops
them. Then I put them in a big
bowl. We made a salad!

My family made fish, carrots, and rice. They are all healthful foods. They taste good, too!

What healthful foods does your family like to eat?

 Connect and Compare

- What does the chart tell you about food?
- What other foods can you think of for each category?

Make a Poster

Writing

✔ **Present-Tense Verbs**

Some verbs tell about actions that happen now.

Amy made a poster about a play.

Grade 1 is in a play.

We sing and dance.

We are so funny!

Come see it.

Your Turn

Suppose your class is putting on a play.

Think about what is special about the play.

Make a poster telling people why the play is special.

Grammar and Writing

- Read Amy's poster.
  Find the **verbs** that tell about now.
  Point to the exclamation mark.

- Check your poster.
  Do you tell why the play is special?
  Do you use **verbs** that tell about what happens now?

- Display your poster.

Talk About It

What types of art do you know about? What kind of art do you like to make?

LOG ON ▶ **VIEW IT**

Oral Language Activities
Making Art
www.macmillanmh.com

66

Making Art

✓ Words to Know

people
every
from
your
into
soon

_____

when
stitch

Make A Doll

Dolls are like **people**. They come in **every** size and shape.

What do you think this doll was made **from**? Yes! It was made from a bit of cloth.

68

You can make a doll with **your** sock. Put some fluff **into** the sock. When the fluff is in, stitch the sock up. **Soon** you can play with your doll!

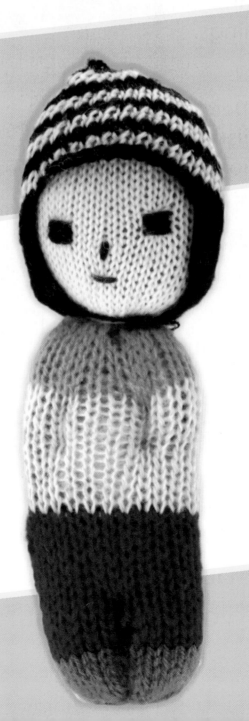

Comprehension

Genre
Nonfiction
A nonfiction article tells about real people and things.

Reread
Main Idea and Details
Look for details that give information about masks.

Masks! Masks! Masks!

A mask hides **your** face. When you put on a mask, you can act out a story. You can act as if you are not yourself.

People make masks in **every** land.
Masks help them tell tales.
And masks help them have fun.

This mask is **from** Africa. What
shapes can you see on the mask?
Which animal is on top?

The masks on this page are from
Japan. People use them when they
act in plays. What tales could they
tell with such masks?

Look at this bird. How do you think this mask was made? What is it made from?

It takes much skill to make such a mask.

This mask is from Peru. It is shaped like the sun. Look at it. Can you see snakes?

Make a Mask

You can make a mask, too! First, get a plate. Cut holes **into** it. Check that you can see.

Next, color the mask. Paste fun things on it. **Soon** you will have a mask!

Last, tape a band on the back of the mask. Put the mask on. Who are you?

 Comprehension Check

Tell What You Learned

What did you learn about making masks?

Think and Compare

1. Name something a mask can help you do.

2. How can you make a mask?

3. What information did you learn in this article? What is it mainly about?

4. Would you rather make a sock doll or a mask? Why?

Test Practice

Answering Questions
Sometimes the answer is on the page. Sometimes it is not. You must look for clues.

Art in Caves

In 1940, four boys saw a hole in the ground. It was a cave.

The boys went in. They saw pictures on the walls. The pictures showed people and animals. There were birds, fish, horses, and bulls.

The boys told people about the caves. Scientists came. They said the pictures were thousands of years old. They showed how early people lived.

DIRECTIONS
Answer the questions.

1 Where were the paintings found?

    Ⓐ In an art museum

    Ⓑ In a building

    Ⓒ In a cave

2 Who found the cave?

    Ⓐ Scientists

    Ⓑ Four boys

    Ⓒ A cat

3 The people who painted the cave paintings —

    Ⓐ lived a long time ago

    Ⓑ are still alive today

    Ⓒ lived in 1940

Write an Invitation

Anthony wrote an invitation to an art show.

Art Show!

Come to our art show.
It will be on Friday.
It is in Ms. Rick's room.
We painted animals.
They are so funny!

The writer included important information.

Write to a Prompt

Plan an art show for your class. Write an invitation. Tell about the show.

Then write when and where the show will be.

Writing Hints

- ☑ Plan what your invitation will say.

- ☑ Tell when and where the show will be.

- ☑ Did I use past and future tense verbs correctly?

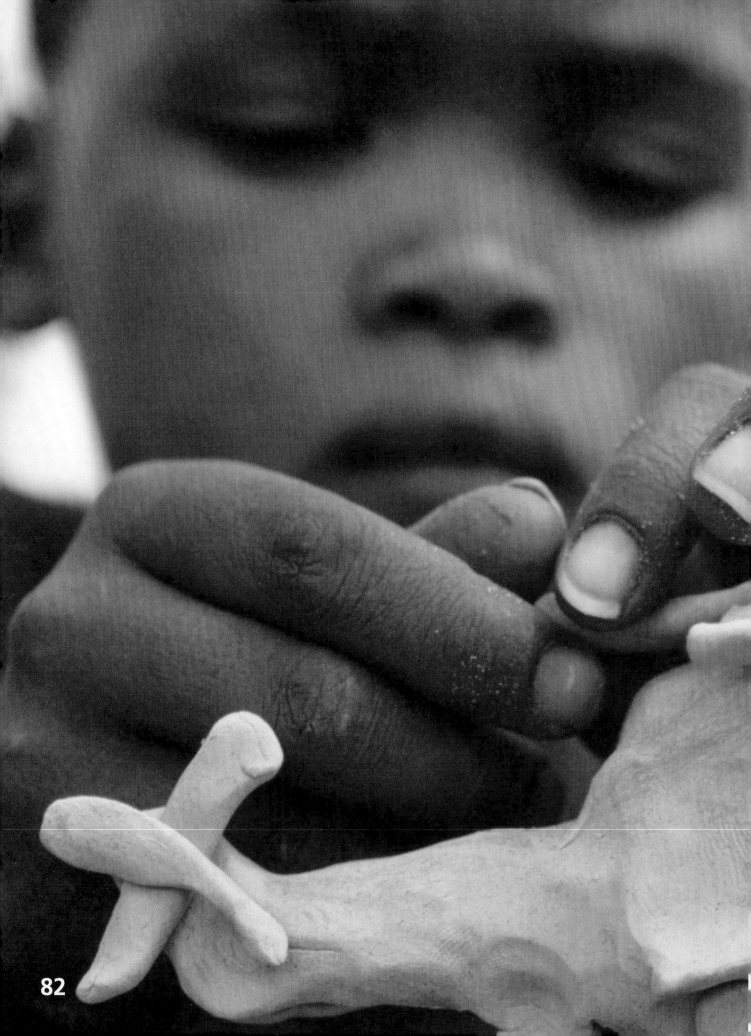

Talk About It

What does it mean to be creative? How are you creative?

LOG ON ▶ **VIEW IT**

Oral Language Activities
Being Creative
www.macmillanmh.com

Being Creative

✔ **Words to Know**

done
old
new
find
work
after

_____

u̲s̲e
ho̲p̲e

Read To Find Out
What will happen to the old box?

The Old Box

"I am **done** with this
old box," said Mom.

84

"Let's save it! We can make a **new** thing with it," said Kim.

"OK," said Mom. "I hope you **find** a nice way to use it!"

85

Kim and Luke went to **work**.
"We can drive this when it's
done," said Luke.

After it was done, Kim and Luke got in. They played with it for a long time. They had fun!

Rose

Genre
A **Fantasy** is a made-up story that could not happen in real life.

Reread
✓ **Draw Conclusions**
Use your Conclusions Chart.

Story Clue	Story Clue

↓

Conclusion

Read to Find Out
Why does Rose Robot like old things?

Robot Cleans Up

by Mary Anderson
illustrated by Michael Garland

89

Rose Robot liked to **find old** things.
Her little brother, Rob, liked to help.

"Rose, what will we do with this old
junk?" asked Rob.

"We will use it," said Rose.

They passed Luke and his dad.

"This stuff broke," said Luke. "We are bringing it to the dump."

"But it is such good stuff!" said Rose. "I can use it."

Luke gave his old stuff to Rose.

Rose and Rob went home.

"Rose, is that more old stuff?" asked her mom.

"What will you do with that junk?" asked her dad.

"I am going to use it," said Rose.

Rose went to her room.

"Come and help me, Rob," she said.
"I will make a **new** toy for you to
jump in."

Soon Rose was **done**.

"Get in, Rob," she said.

"Rose! Look at me jump!" said Rob.
"You make the best things."

"What is that thumping?" asked Mom.

"What is going on up there?" asked Dad.

"Let's go find out," they said.

"Rob! Stop that jumping!" said Mom.

"Rose! Look at this mess," said Dad.

Then Mom and Dad spoke together. "We must get rid of all this junk," they said.

"But this is such good stuff!" said Rose.
"Look! I made this for reading in bed."

"And she made this for me to play a
tune on!" said Rob.

"Very cute," said Mom. "But this mess has to go!"

"Tomorrow we will bring the things you can't use to the dump," said Dad.

98

After Mom and Dad left, Rose looked at her stuff.

"Rob, I have a plan," said Rose. "I can have a clean room and still keep my stuff."

"Can I help?" asked Rob.

Rose and Rob went to **work**.

"We can use so much of this stuff," said Rose.

"I hope Mom and Dad like this!" said Rob.

Rose and Rob worked and worked.

At last, they were done. Rose smiled.

"This is my best thing yet," she said.

"I'll get Mom and Dad," said Rob.

"Mom and Dad!" said Rob. "Look at what we made."

"What is it?" they asked.

"You'll see," said Rose. "I just have to pull this knob."

"Your room is so clean!" said Mom.

"And you used so much old stuff," said Dad.

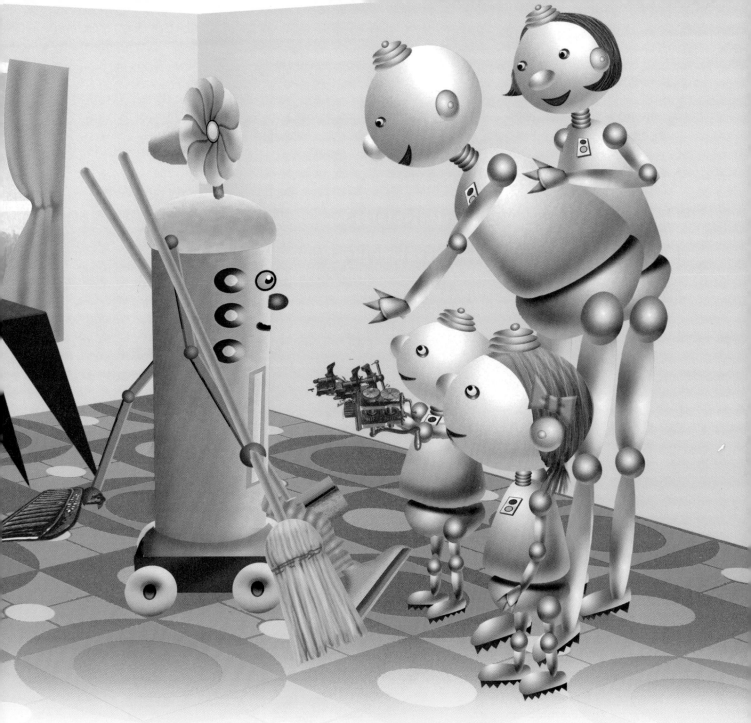

"Look!" said Rob. "This is the stuff we didn't use. You can bring it to the dump."

"But Rose can make something new with it," said Mom and Dad.

"I can!" said Rose.

Who Made Rose Robot?

Mary Anderson says, "I am just like Rose Robot. I love to find old stuff. My home is filled with things I have found and fixed up."

Michael Garland paints, draws, and uses a computer to make his pictures.

Other books by Michael Garland

LOG ON ▶ FIND OUT

Author Mary Anderson
Illustrator Michael Garland
www.macmillanmh.com

✔ Author's Purpose

Mary Anderson tells about an unusual machine. Write about a machine you'd like to make.

106

Comprehension Check

Retell the Story

Use the Retelling Cards to retell the story in order.

Retelling Cards

Think and Compare

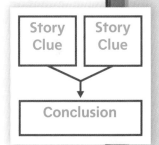

Story Clue	Story Clue
Conclusion	

1. What does Rose Robot like to do?

2. What does Rose Robot do after Mom and Dad tell her to clean up her room?

3. How do Mom and Dad feel about Rose's invention?

4. How is Rose Robot like Kim and Luke in "The Old Box"?

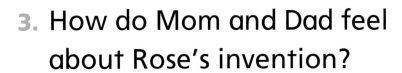

READ TOGETHER

A Bottle Takes a Trip

Ahh! You just drank some water. Now you toss the bottle in a blue bin for **recycling**. What will happen to that bottle?

A truck will come to pick up your bottle. It will go with many bottles to a recycling center.

When they get there, the bottles go down a big slide.

Now people **sort** the cans, bottles, and paper.

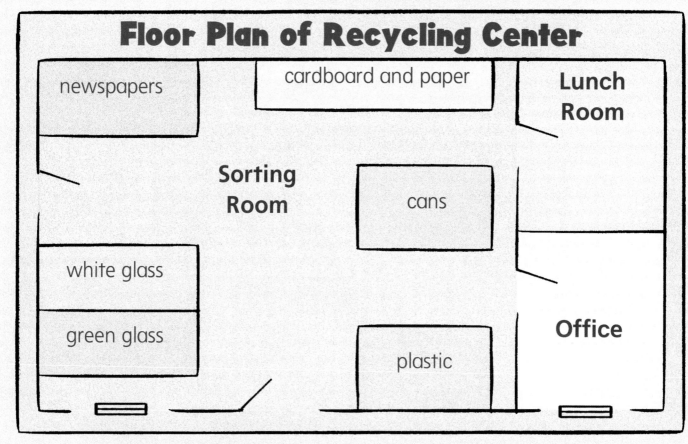

Floor Plan of Recycling Center

newspapers

cardboard and paper

Lunch Room

Sorting Room

cans

white glass

green glass

plastic

Office

Look at this floor plan of a recycling center. What kinds of things do you see being recycled?

Your bottle is made of **plastic**.
It will go to a factory. Here the
bottles are cut up into small bits.

Next the plastic bits are melted until they are soft. The soft plastic can be used to make many new things.

The green rulers on this page were made from recycled plastic. Recycled plastic can also be made into yarn. It can be used to make socks and sweaters and to fill sleeping bags.

All of the things this girl has were made out of recycled plastic. One of them could have come from your bottle!

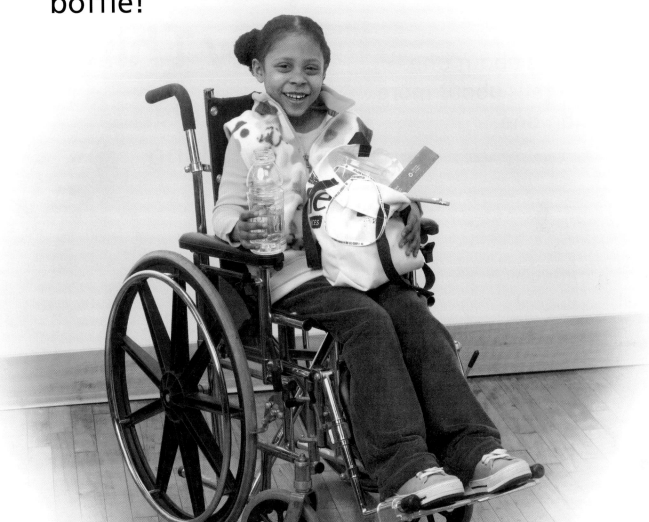

✔ **Connect and Compare**

- How is what Rose Robot does like the recycling in "A Bottle Takes a Trip"?
- What recycled things does the girl in the picture have?

Write About Making a New Thing

Ramon wrote about making a drum.

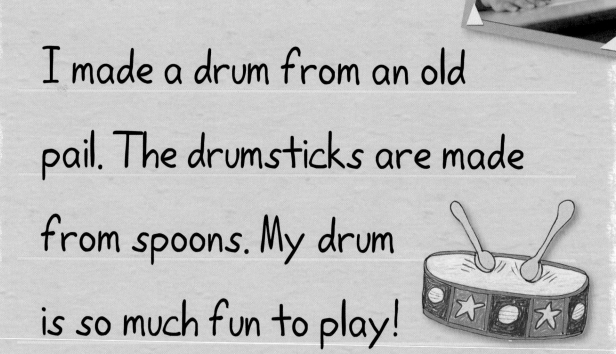

I made a drum from an old pail. The drumsticks are made from spoons. My drum is so much fun to play!

114

Your Turn

What could you make from something old?

Write about it.

Tell how you could make it.

Grammar and Writing

- Read Ramon's writing.
  Point to the words is and are.
  What word does the verb is tell about?
  What word does the verb are tell about?

- Check your writing.
  Do you tell about something you made?
  Do you use is and are correctly?

- Read your description to a partner.

Talk About It

How are children from other places like you? How are they different?

LOG ON ▶ VIEW IT

Oral Language Activities
Kids Around the World
www.macmillanmh.com

Kids Around the World

It's Fun to Help

Kids everywhere like to help. This **boy does** the dishes. He scrubs and splashes. Will he spill **any water**?

This **girl** helps her mom bake.
It smells good. It will taste just
as good!

This boy digs and digs. He will make
a path. He likes to do it **by** himself.

These **friends** help with old cans and glass. They put them into bins.

Helping is fun! What do you do to help?

Comprehension

Genre
Nonfiction tells about real people and things.

Reread
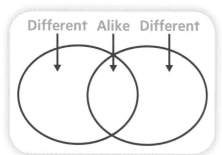
Compare and Contrast
Use your Compare and Contrast Chart.

Different Alike Different

Read to Find Out
How do kids around the world have fun?

Kids Have Fun!

By Minda Novek

Kids have fun in every land.
They have fun doing many things.

It's fun to play games.
Kids in this icy land like
to jump rope.

This **boy** plays a game with a flat bat.
Will he strike the ball?
Do you play **any** games with a bat?

It's fun to move.
This **girl** has lots of fun with a hoop.
When she swings her hips,
the hoop spins.

This boy **does** tricks with a rope.
He can make a ring with it.
Then he jumps into it and out again.

It is fun to make things!
This boy cuts up scraps.
Snip, snip!
What shape did he make?

This girl makes things from leaves.
She cuts them in strips.
She will use them to make a box.

It's fun to make things up.
This boy acts like a lion.
He shakes his mane.
But then he smiles.

These kids like to make up games.
They made a ship.
They used sticks, cloth, and a box.

It's fun to see new things.
This boy finds new things under **water**.
Look at what he picked up!

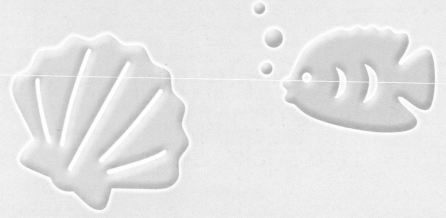

What does this boy see?
It is wide.
How wide can he stretch?

It's fun to learn new things.
This girl's mom shows her
how to make a rug from string.

This boy's dad shows him how to
make pots.
They have fun doing it together.

Holidays are fun!
This boy is all dressed up.
He has a mask.
He acts strong.

These kids get dressed up for a holiday.
Then they have fun dancing.
It's fun to see them!

It's fun to do things with **friends**.
When two kids race like this,
can they go fast?

It's fun to do things **by** yourself.
Just sitting and thinking can be fun.
This girl likes to read.

**Lots of things are fun.
How do you have fun?**

Minda Novek's World

Minda Novek says, "In my books, I like to write about how people live all over the world. I use pictures of real people. I try to show how their lives are like yours and how they are different, too."

LOG ON ▶ FIND OUT
Author Minda Novek
www.macmillanmh.com

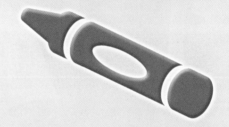

✔ Author's Purpose

Minda Novek wanted to write about how kids all over the world have fun. Write about how you could have fun with a kid from *Kids Have Fun!*

Comprehension Check

Retell the Selection

Use the Retelling Cards to retell the selection in order.

Retelling Cards

Think and Compare

1. What do kids use to make a ship?

2. What do kids have fun doing by themselves? What do they have fun doing with others?

3. What do the two children learn to do with their parents? How is what they are doing the same and different?

4. How are *Kids Have Fun!* and "It's Fun to Help" the same?

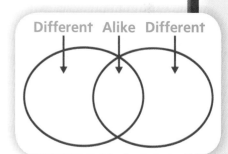

Different Alike Different

Genre
Poems use words in imaginative ways.

✔ **Literary Elements**
Sensory Language
Poets often use words that describe the way something looks, feels, tastes, sounds, or smells.

Alliteration is when the same beginning sound in a group of words is repeated.

LOG ON ▶ FIND OUT

Poetry Fun with Words
www.macmillanmh.com

Kids' Poems From Around the World

Kids everywhere write poetry. These kids found new ways to write about the sky, the sea, and the sun.

The Sky Is Busy

The lighthouse
On that island
Is shining.
Helicopters in the sky
Are shining.
Boats are glittering, too.
And with a bang
Someone is shooting
off fireworks.
Today the sky
Is very busy.

Ishikawa Mwumi,
Kindergarten, Japan

The Sea

The mist smudges out
Kapiti Island

the hills curve and rise
like loaves of bread

the sun sprinkles glitter
on the sea

the wind is writing what it knows
in lines along the water.

Laura Ranger, age 7,
New Zealand

Sun Rise

Sun, sun, sun
Rise up from the clouds
Spread your rays
Flowers will be happy
Birds will sing
And I shall be happy
and sing, too.

Camille Pabalan,
age 6, Canada

✔ **Connect and Compare**

- What words describe the way something looks and sounds?
- What lines in "The Sea" have words that begin with the same sounds?

145

Writing

✔ Contractions

A **contraction** is a short form of two words.

is + not = isn't

Write About Fun at School

Wren wrote about playing statues.

I like to play *statues.*

When Miss Chan tells us to

stop, we can't move.

It isn't easy but it's fun!

146

Your Turn

How do you have fun at school?

Write about it.

Tell what you do and why you like it.

Grammar and Writing

- Read Wren's writing.
  Point to each contraction.
  Name the two words that each contraction stands for.

- Check your writing.
  Do you describe a fun thing at school?
  Do you use contractions correctly?

- Read your writing to a partner.

Kate and June

Review

Make Predictions
Main Idea and Details
Photographs
Labels

June　　　　　**Kate**

 Kate: Can you play with me, June?

June: OK. But I don't have much time.

 Kate: I 'd like to swing in the park.

148

June: It takes such a long time to get there.

 Kate: What do you want to do?

 **June:** I want to ride bikes.

 Kate: If we ride, we can get to the park fast.

 **June:** Good thinking, Kate.

 Kate: Now we can swing and ride!

Made at Home

Today kids shop for toys and games. What did kids do long ago? A lot of kids made toys at home. They used things they could find.

Kids made kites at home. They used bags, sticks, and string.

Kids made dolls from cloth. They cut out shapes. They stuffed them with rags. Then they stitched them up. Kids made dolls from lots of things. They even used corn husks!

Today kids hit balls with a bat. A long time ago, kids made bats from big sticks. What did they call the game? They called it stick ball!

homemade kite

corn husk doll

Show What You Know

 Word Study

Past, Present, or Future?

- Read each verb below. Does it tell about the past, present, or future?

  jump   hopped   will kick   baked

- Pick one verb.

- Use the verb in sentences that tell about the past, present, and future.

 Phonics

Make And Read Words

- Start with the word robe.

- Change b to d.

- Change o to u.

- Change u to i.

- Change r to h.

- What are the new words?

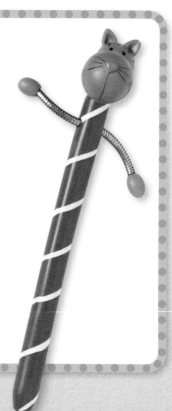

Comprehension

A Fun How-To

- Think of something fun you know how to make. Write the steps.

- Add pictures and symbols that show what to use and what to do.

- Help a classmate use your How-To. Talk about what the symbols mean.

Writing

See Sam Sit by the Sea

- Write a poem with alliteration. Think of words that begin with that sound.

- Write a short poem. Use some of your same-sound words near each other.

- Your poem could be about something fun or silly. Draw a picture to go with your poem. Share it with the class.

Glossary

What Is a Glossary?

A glossary can help you find the meanings of words. The words are listed in alphabetical order. You can look up a word and read it in a sentence. There is a picture to help you.

old

friends

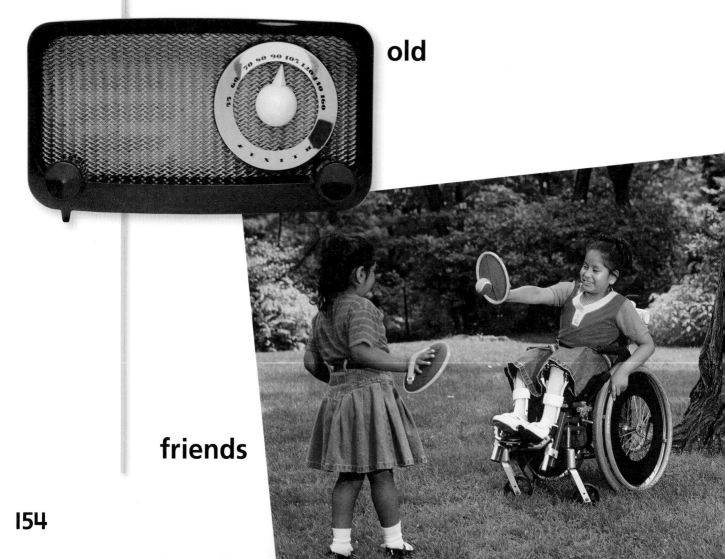

Sample Entry

Letter

Main Entry

Sentence

B b

bus

We take the **bus** to school.

duck

Bb

boy

This **boy** likes to jump rope.

bubbles

The **bubbles** are colorful.

bus

We take the **bus** to school.

Cc

cute

Meg has a **cute** kitten.

Dd

duck

The **duck** is floating on the pond.

Ff

friends

I have fun with my **friends**.

Ll

lake

The boat is on the **lake**.

like

Most cats don't **like** dogs.

Mm

make

Grace can **make** dolls from old socks.

Oo

old

This radio is very **old**.

Pp

path

We walk on the **path**.

plastic

I have a **plastic** lunch box.

Rr

rope

Rose and Jess can climb a **rope**.

Ss

scrubs

Scott **scrubs** the dishes.

Tt

together

Katie and Matt build **together**.

Ww

wig

I wear a **wig**.

Acknowledgments

The publisher gratefully acknowledges permission to reprint the following copyrighted material:

"The Sea" by Laura Ranger from poems from *Stone Soup Magazine* May/June 1993 issue. Copyright © 2005 by Stone Soup, Santa Cruz, CA 95063.

"The Sky is Busy" by Ishikawa Megumi © 1993 from *Festival in My Heart: Poems by Japanese Children*, Harry N. Abrams, Incorporated, NY, A Times Mirror Corporations. Reprinted with permission from Harry N. Abrams, Inc., NY.

"Sun Rise" by Camille Pabalan from *KidzPage: Poetry and Verse for Children of All Ages*, November 2000, page 36, Tangled Lives. Copyright © 1998–2000 by Emmi Tarr.

Book Cover, MRS. BROWN WENT TO TOWN by Wong Herbert Yee. Copyright © 2003 by Wong Herbert Yee. Reprinted by permission of Houghton Mifflin.

Book Cover, CIRCUS GIRL by Michael Garland. Copyright © 1993 by Michael Garland. Used by permission of Dutton Children's Books, a division of Penguin Books USA Inc.

Book Cover, FIREMAN SMALL by Wong Herbert Yee. Copyright © 1994 by Wong Herbert Yee. Reprinted by permission of Houghton Mifflin Company.

ILLUSTRATIONS

Cover Illustration: Pablo Bernasconi

8–11: Vincent Nguyen. 12–29: Wong Herbert Yee. 30–33: Mircea Catusanu. 34: Ken Bowser. 35: Diane Paterson. 38–41: Anthony Lewis. 42-59: G. Brian Karas. 76: K. Michael Crawford. 80: Julia Woolf. 84–87: Josée Masse. 88–107: Michael Garland. 108–112: Jessica Wolk Stanley. 114: Daniel DelValle. 142–145: Tomek Bogacki. 146: Ken Bowser. 148–149: Elivia Savadier. 156-157, 159–160: Carol Koeller. 163: Janee Trasler.

PHOTOGRAPHY

All photographs are by Ken Cavanagh or Ken Karp or Natalie Ray for Macmillan/McGraw Hill (MMH) except as noted below.

iv: David R. Stoecklein/drsphoto.net. v: (t) The Art Archive/Neil Setchfield; (b) Sean Justice/Getty Images. 2–3: David R. Stoecklein/drsphoto.net. 4: Rubberball/PunchStock. 4–5: Farinaz Taghavi/Getty Images. 5: Richard Nowitz/Getty Images. 6–7: Tim Fitzharris/Masterfile. 28: Courtesy of Wong Herbert Yee. 30: (bl) SW Productions/Getty Images; (bcl) Comstock Images/Alamy; (bcr) simplestockshots/PunchStock; (br) Royalty-Free/CORBIS. 31: Richard Hutchings/Photo Edit. 32: (tl) Dave Nagel/Getty Images; (tr) David Frazier/Corbis. 33: (tl) Stockbyte/PunchStock; (cr) Mixa/PunchStock. 34: Bill Frymire/Masterfile. 36–37: Myrleen Ferguson Cate/PhotoEdit. 58: Courtesy of Aida Marcuse. 60: Ace Stock Limited/Alamy. 60–63: (bkgd) Wetzel and Company. 61: (t) D. Hurst/Alamy; (bcr) PhotoLink/Getty Images; (br) Digital Vision/Getty Images. 62: (t) Blend/PunchStock; (cr) John A. Rizzo/Getty Images; (bl) C Squared Studios/Getty Images. 63: Studio M/Stock Connection/Jupiter Images. 64: Ariel Skelly/Corbis. 65: (tcr) Photodisc/Getty Images; (tr) Hemera Technologies/Alamy. 66–67: The Art Archive/Neil Setchfield. 68: Gail Vachon. 69: Jim Lane/Alamy. 70: (tr) Brooklyn Museum/Corbis; (bl) Scala/Art Resource. 71: Jon Arnold Images/Alamy. 72: Giraudon/Art Resource. 73: Scala/Art Resource. 74: Frans Lanting/Corbis. 75: Brooklyn Museum/Corbis. 78: Maxppp/Zuma Press/Newscom. 80: Royalty-Free/Corbis. 81: (br) C Squared Studios/Getty Images; (c) Dian Lofton. 82–83: Anthony Bannister/Corbis. 106: (tr) Courtesy of Mary Anderson; (cl) Courtesy of Michael Garland. 108: Ken Karp/Macmillan McGraw-Hill. 109: Javier Larrea/AGE Fotostock. 110: AP Images/Rich Pedroncelli. 111–112: Richard Hutchings/Photo Edit. 113: Ken Karp/Macmillan McGraw-Hill. 114: LWA-Dann Tardif/Corbis. 115: Natalie Ray for MMH. 116–117: Bryan & Cherry Alexander Photography. 118: Van Hilversum/Alamy. 119: Paul Chesley/Getty Images. 120: David Morris/Alamy. 121: Bob Daemmrich/The Image Works. 122: Sean Justice/Getty Images. 124: Robert van der Hilst/Corbis. 125: Karan Kapoor/Getty Images. 126: Digital Vision/Getty Images. 127: Lindsay Hebberd/Corbis. 128: Photodisc/PunchStock . 129: Bob Krist/Corbis. 130: Rebecca Emery/Corbis. 131: Digital Vision/Getty Images. 132: Terje Rakke/Getty Images. 133: Randy Faris/Corbis. 134: Paul Chesley/Getty Images. 135: Alvaro Leiva/AGE Fotostock. 136: Rodolfo Arpia/Alamy. 137: Robert Fried/Alamy. 138: Dennis MacDonald/AGE Fotostock. 139: Avril O'Reilly/Alamy. 140: Courtesy of Minda Novek. 146: Bohemian Nomad Picturemakers/Corbis. 147: Nic Hamilton / Alamy. 150: Enzo & Paolo Ragazzini/Corbis. 151: (br) Sherman/Getty Images; (bc) David Lassman/Syracuse Newspapers/The Image Works; (tr) C Squared Studios/Getty Images. 152: Ken Cavanagh/Macmillan/McGraw-Hill. 153: Stephen Ogilvy/Macmillan McGraw-Hill. 154: (cl) Photodisc/Getty Images; (br) Laura Dwight/Corbis. 155: (t) Gary Buss/Getty Images; (b) Getty Images. 156: Bill Hickey/Getty Images. 157: Gary Buss/Getty Images. 158: (t) Getty Images; (b) Tom & Dee Ann McCarthy/Corbis. 159: Tim Davis/Corbis. 160: Photodisc/Getty Images. 161: Stockbyte/Picture Quest. 162: (t) Joyce Choo/Corbis; (b) Jennie Woodcock/Reflections Photolibrary/Corbis. 163: Joseph Sohm/ChromoSohm Inc./Corbis.